FIVE SHORT PLAYS

A COLLECTION WRITTEN BY KAREN CARSON

FIVE SHORT PLAYS, A COLLECTION WRITTEN BY KAREN CARSON
consists of:

  101 Channels, a Comedy Short (2 older characters)
  Side Effects, a Comedy Short (2 characters,
      plus 4 - 7 non-speaking roles)
  Grandma's Kitchen, a Short Horror (2 characters)
  The Cylinder, a Radio Play Thriller (2 characters)
  The Parting, a dramatic play (2 older characters)

"A HUNDRED AND ONE CHANNELS"

A Short Comedy Play

By Karen Carson

"A HUNDRED AND ONE CHANNELS"

The scene takes place in a living room. GERTY is seated on a couch, Center Stage, facing the audience. She is munching on a bowl of popcorn that she holds.

Momentarily, HERB joins her.

They are both seated the whole time, facing the audience which is in the direction of the television set that GERTY and HERB watch.

They are both dressed casually, and sit comfortably, for a night of TV watching.

HERB: What's on tonight?

GERTY: I don't know off-hand.

HERB: I'll just flip through the channels.

GERTY: O.k.

HERB *picks up remote.*

As HERB flips through the channels with the remote, they both look forward, as if seeing television shows pass by. There are frequent, unspecified pauses, as the channels are being changed.

HERB *starts changing channels. After about three channels …*

GERTY: Wait, what was that?

HERB: What, this?

GERTY: No, back another one.

HERB: This?

GERTY: Another one.

HERB: I went back another one!

GERTY: Aw, forget it. Just keep goin'.

HERB: Thank you. *(Operates remote again)*

GERTY: Ooh-ooh, what was that?!

HERB: No, no! That was that stupid chick-flick that we, by the way, agreed <u>not</u> to watch.

GERTY: Oh.

HERB *keeps flipping through channels.*

GERTY: Why did we agree not to watch it again?

HERB: 'Cause I don't wanna watch it.

GERTY: But it's probably a good movie …

HERB: They say it's a tear-jerker. And you know how I hate it when you cry.

GERTY: What did you just pass there?

HERB: Oh, God! *(Stops flipping through channels, looks at her, annoyed)*

GERTY: Well, what's the sense of flippin' through channels, if we're not seein' what we're missin'?

HERB: If we're not seein' what we're missin', then we ain't missin' it.

GERTY: But I don't know what I'm missin', 'cause you're not lettin' me see it!

HERB: *(Handing her the remote)* You wanna flip through 'em?

GERTY: No, you like doin' that. *(Goes back to her popcorn)*

HERB: Thank you. *(Starts flipping through again)*

GERTY: Oh, God!

HERB: What? What?!

GERTY: That was George Clooney!

HERB: So? Who's George Clooney?

GERTY: "Who's George Clooney"!

HERB: What, is he related to Rosemary Clooney?

GERTY: He's a sex symbol, that's what!

HERB: Is he related to Rosemary Clooney!

GERTY: I don't know!

HERB: Then I don't care. *(Flipping through again)*

GERTY: What about that?

HERB: What about it?

GERTY: Well, it's dolphins, or something.

HERB: Exactly. *(Keeps flipping)*

GERTY: Well, it's nature! Don't you wanna watch nature?!

HERB: No. Not unless it involves breasts.

GERTY: You're a pig, Herb.

HERB: Thank you, Gerty. *(Keeps flipping)*

GERTY: How many channels is this so far?

HERB: How should I know?

GERTY: Well, we're payin' for 100 channels, and …

HERB: A hundred and one.

GERTY: A hundred and one, and I ain't seen one yet!

HERB: We got more to go.

GERTY: But I'm not seein' anything on any of 'em!

HERB: There's nothin' on!

GERTY: How can you know that?!

HERB: Because I'm lookin' as I'm flippin'!

GERTY: O.k. O.k. If you're lookin' as you're flippin', then what did we just pass?

HERB: I don't know.

GERTY: Stop! What did it look like?

HERB: *(Stops, sighs)* Like a game show, Gerty.

GERTY: Right! It was Wheel of Fortune! And you passed it!

HERB: A hundred channels and we gotta watch Wheel?!

GERTY: A hundred and one! And there's nothin' else on!

HERB: How do you know?! I'm the one who's flippin'!

GERTY: I know, 'cause you're the one who's flippin'!

HERB: Look, let me just see what else is on, o.k.?

GERTY *sighs, as* HERB *continues to flip through channels.*

GERTY: There! There! That's that new reality show!

HERB: We <u>definitely</u> ain't watchin' that.

GERTY: Why not! These people got to get to the next island, or else they gotta eat a slug.

HERB: We're not watchin' that!

GERTY: There's boobs in it!

HERB: *(Short pause, as he thinks about it)* Alright, if nothin' else is on, we'll go back to that.

GERTY: You're a pig, Herb.

HERB: Thank you, Gerty. *(Continues to flip through)*

GERTY: Wait! The Golden Girls!

HERB: Aw, fer gosh sakes, Gerty! We've watched all o' them ten times each!

GERTY: And I never get tired of them.

HERB: Well, I do!

GERTY: They're funny!

HERB: They're boring!

GERTY: Blanche is sexy!

HERB: She's old!

GERTY: The mother's histerical!

HERB: The mother is dead! And so is the other one! And so is the show! *(Flips through with a vengeance)*

GERTY: How 'bout some news?

HERB: What do you wanna hear bad stuff for?

GERTY: I don't! I wanna laugh with the Golden Girls!

HERB: Hey, there's a hockey match …

GERTY: Don't _even_ think about it.

HERB: I do like sports.

GERTY: Then go back about five channels. There was figure skating on.

HERB: Figure skating is not a sport!

GERTY: Can you do it?

HERB: No.

GERTY: Then it's a sport.

HERB: I'm not watchin' guys in tights.

GERTY: Guess that's why we passed the ballet, too, a few channels ago.

HERB: You got that right!

GERTY: There! What about the weather?

HERB *looks out the window, Stage Left.*

HERB: It's dark out and raining.

GERTY: What about tomorrow's weather?!

HERB: I could die tonight flippin' channels. I'll worry about tomorrow's weather tomorrow.

GERTY *scoffs, disgusted.*

HERB: They're always wrong anyway. Hey, what about this?

GERTY: A cooking show?!

HERB: Oh, geez, is that what that is?

GERTY: You saw breasts, and a cheesecake! And that's what interests you?!

HERB: I only saw the breasts.

GERTY: You're a pig, Herb.

HERB: Thank you, Gerty.

GERTY: I want my own TV.

CURTAIN

"SIDE EFFECTS"

A Short Comedy Play

by, Karen Carson

"SIDE EFFECTS"

SCENE
(Classroom setting)

An Orientation session is about to begin for a group
of newly hired employees (the hirees) into a sales
department.

SANDY BARSTOW is setting up at the front desk of the
classroom to speak at the Orientation meeting.

BETH STRATTON, her superior, enters.

                    BETH
Hello, Ms. Barstow! Oh, good! I see you're getting ready!

                    SANDY
Oh, hi, Beth! Please call me Sandy.

                    BETH
Oh, very well. But just for your info, the new hirees
should call you Ms. Barstow. It's just more formal and
respectable.

                    SANDY
Oh, sure! I'm so excited about this, really!

                    BETH
So, this is your first time speaking at orientation, isn't
that right?

                    SANDY
Yes! Yes, it is!

                    BETH
Do you have any questions?

                    SANDY
No. No, I think I can handle it alright.

                    BETH
Great! You certainly look ready!

                              SANDY

Well, I was so excited last night, I really didn't get much
sleep at all, so I woke up with a bit of a headache. And a
backache, as well. I also have a bit of a cold, but no
worry. I took something for it.

                              BETH

Well, good.

                              SANDY

Yeah. I discovered a new all-day, mucus-taming, snot
bubble-blocking, headache calming, wide-awake, throat
tickle tamer so you can speak at Orientation medicine.

                              BETH

I-I see. Well, I hope it works.

                              SANDY

Oh, yeah, it always does. Of course, just to be safe, I
took something to stay "focused," if you will. And a little
something for the arthritic back, too.

                              BETH

Oh.

                              SANDY

I just didn't want any of that to get in the way. And I
also have hay fever, so, ya know, didn't want to risk a
sneezing attack.

                              BETH

Oh. Are you supposed to take all those things together?

                              SANDY

Well, I never take anything I don't need, see. So, today,
well, I needed 'em all.

                              BETH

Well, I guess it's o.k.

                              SANDY

Oh, sure, I'm fine!

                              BETH
                           (jokingly)
As long as you're not operating any heavy machinery, right?

                        SANDY
Yeah! Yeah, right, Beth.
                (gets stuck at the "TH" sound in "Beth," as
                if her tongue is swelling.)
Beth-th-th!

                        BETH
What?

                        SANDY
Oh. Oh, nothing. It's nothing.
                (playing with the word on her tongue)
Noth-th-th-ing. Noth-th-ing.

                        BETH
Are you sure you're gonna be alright?

                        SANDY
Oh, yeah, yeah! No sweat! Really.

                        BETH
Well, o.k.
                (way out of character)
Because your ass looks so bitchin' in that tight skirt, I
can hardly hold my hands back! Ha!

                        SANDY
Wh-what?! What?!

                        BETH
What?

                        SANDY
What did you just say?!

                        BETH
I said, "As soon as you hear the bell ring, the meeting
will start."

                        SANDY
You said *that?!*

                        BETH
Yes! What did you think I said?

                        SANDY
Noth-thing. Noth-thing.

                              BETH
Now, there are just a few new hires this morning, so it
shouldn't be difficult to keep their attention.

                              SANDY
Oh. Right.

                              BETH
Before you know it, it'll be break time. So, I'll leave
you now. Good luck!

                              SANDY
                    (a little worried now)
Thanks. Yeah.
                    (continues sorting her papers)

     The BELL RINGS.

                              SANDY
                    (about jumping out of her skin)
Oh, Lord, what's that?!!
                    (pause, calming herself)
Oh. Oh, it's that bell. Right.

     SANDY turns to the black board behind her and starts
     writing her name. She writes "SANDY," then hesitates.

     The new hirees (4 – 7 of them) quietly start filing in.
     They sit anywhere, and their attention is on SANDY.

                              SANDY
                    (still with back to classroom, to self)
Sandy. Sandy … God, what the hell is my last name?!
                    (beat)
Aw, screw it!

SANDY writes "BEACH" after her first name.

                              SANDY
                    (amused at her "new name")
Sandy Beach! Ha-ha! Yeah, Sandy Beach …

     SANDY turns to face classroom, and screams at the
     sight of the people. They all scream or yelp in
     surprise, as well, then worriedly look at each other.

SANDY

Oh, oh, sorry!
                    (trying to laugh it off)
I thought you were all … er, something else.

    Beat, as hirees look to each other for an explanation.

SANDY

O.k., so, welcome to Orientation. And congratulations on
your new sales positions at Golden Homes Décor Company.
You've all already met some of the staff, and during your
first weeks working for Golden Homes, I'm sure you'll find
that the company is unfair, prejudiced, and management
really sucks the big one.

    The new hirees are appalled, as they look at each
    other, a bit confused and angry now.

SANDY

But no worries! You'll soon learn that a little ass-
kissing and boot-licking will turn your future right around,
and you'll be headed for some kind of menial middle-
management job yourselves.
                    (laughs a little)

    BETH enters to check on the class. She quickly loses
    her optimistic smile.

SANDY

Now. Everybody, let's see how you lick. I want everyone
to go like this.
                    (sticks tongue out, as she chants)
La-la-la-la-la-la …

    BETH stops SANDY, pulling her aside and speaking in a
    loud whisper.

BETH

What are you doing?!

SANDY

Oh, hi! No worries, really! I know this is not part of
the scheduled criteria.

BETH

Of course it isn't!

                              SANDY

I haven't gotten there yet. I just decided to open with a
joke, that's all.

                              BETH

A joke?

                              SANDY

Yes. You know, to get their attention. To bond, if you
will. Just look at their faces.

     Hirees look confused, smile nervously.

                              BETH

Well, alright. But get to it, Ms. Barstow! Stay on topic!

                              SANDY

Yes! Yes, I will, …

     BETH leaves.

                              SANDY
                    (after her)
… Beth-th-th.
                    (to class)
O.k., where were we?
                    (beat)
Aw, who cares?
                    (referring to black board)
O.k., my name is …
                    (can hardly contain herself)
Sandy Beach!!

     Hirees laugh.

                              SANDY
                    (immediately gets serious)
But you are all to call me Ms. Beach!
                    (beat, strictly)
                              SANDY (cont'd)
Does everyone understand that?!

     Hirees nod heads "yes."

                         SANDY
Good. I'm glad somebody does. Now, according to my …
                    (tries to focus on paperwork)
… blurred instructions, … uh, I'm supposed to start off
with ethics. So, that's where we'll start.
                    (focuses on class)
Poppycock!

          Hirees jump, surprised again.

                         SANDY
That's right! I said it! This company has no ethics!
That's why I'm here. I'm uneth-th-th-ical!
                    (jumps back, as if she sees something flying
                     around her head)
Aah! Aah! What was that?!
                    (gets it together)
O.k. That there … that was apparently nothing, uh …

          Hirees react. They are confused.

                         SANDY
Now …
                    (beat)
… as soon as the room stops spinning around, I'll continue
with the Orientation.

          SANDY loses her balance, falls to ground, gets up
          immediately, as hirees laugh, realizing she's high as
          a kite.

                         SANDY
                    (amused)
What happened? Did somebody tell a joke?

          They're all laughing now, as BETH enters.

                         BETH
                    (interrupting)
Uh, Ms. Barstow? Can I speak to you for a moment?

                         SANDY
Ha-ha! Oh, yes, yes!
                    (to class)
Carry on! I'll be right back.

                    BETH pulls her aside.

                              BETH
                         (controlled)
          Is everything alright, Sandy?

                              SANDY
          Oh, yes! You know, this group of hirees is gonna be just
          great! I've already informed them about how this company
          operates, and they know just what they have to do to get
          ahead, ya know what I mean?

                              BETH
          Really? Already?

                              SANDY
          Oh, yeah. I've got it together. We're bonding, and this
          group is gonna surprise you, I'm sure.

                              BETH
          Well, that's remarkable, Sandy! I'm so glad!

                              SANDY
          Yeah, yeah!

                              BETH
          Good job!

                              SANDY
          Thank you!

                              BETH
          Well, you're so much ahead of schedule now, …
                         (to class)
          … why don't we take a break?

                    Hirees stand, leave their desks, and exit.

                              BETH
          So, you're feeling good for the second half of Orientation?

                              SANDY
          Yes! Oh, yes!
                         (beat)
          But, I do have to remark about something.

BETH
(attentively)
Oh, yes, yes, of course!

SANDY
O.k. Uh. Not that I care, or anything, but … those purple kangaroos in the corner? … wearing the capes? … in the rhinestone Elton John sunglasses and the spats? … were they invited to this Orientation?

CURTAIN

"GRANDMA'S KITCHEN"

A Short Horror Play

By, Karen Carson

"GRANDMA'S KITCHEN"

SCENE ONE
(A suburban neighborhood. Birds are
chirping, and there is gentle breeze
on this autumn day, so we can hear the
rustle of the colorful, crisp tree
leaves.)

(TAMMY, a 19-year old student, arrives
at her grandmother's house, and she is
about to use her key to unlock the
cottage-type home, but she finds that
it is unlocked.)

                    TAMMY
Hmm.

     (She goes in.)

                    TAMMY
          (calling out)
Hello?! Grandma?! Anybody home?!

     (A stuffed animal cat stands near the entrance,
     looking up at Tammy.)

                    TAMMY
Hey, Snagglepuss?
          (pets it, giggling a little)
Where's your momma, huh?
          (looks, walking into living room, then calls)
Grandma?

     (In the living room there are perhaps twenty stuffed
     animal cats all posed and on every piece of furniture,
     as well as the floor.)

                    TAMMY
          (to self)
Grandma, you and your stuffed cats.

                          TAMMY
                    (Calling out)
Grandma, it's Wednesday! I'm taking you to the store,
remember?

          (TAMMY opens a cabinet door and is startled by yet
          another stuffed animal cat in such a peculiar place.)

                          TAMMY
Grandma! I think you need a hobby.
                    (joking, nervously)
This one looks hungry.

          (Makes her way past some other cats to the kitchen.
          Sniffs at the air. Looks down to see an empty cat
          food dish.)

                          TAMMY
Well, you guys don't have any food, no wonder you're
staring at me.
                    (calls out)
Hey, Grandma! You feedin' the fake cats now?
                    (laughs, nervously)
Maybe she got a real one. I hope she got a real one.

          (Tammy looks in a couple of cupboards, finds some cat
          food and fills the dish.)

Here, Kitty!

                          TAMMY
                    (talking to some stuffed animal cats on the
                    countertop)
From the smell of things, your cat box probably needs
cleaning, too.
                    (calling out)
Grandma, I have a class at 2:00, I gotta get going!
                    (sighs, as she sees the cat box.)
In the kitchen? Really?

          (Suddenly, there is BANG coming from another room.)

                          TAMMY
                    (calling, a bit impatiently now)
Grandma? Are you ready to go?!

                    (TAMMY scoops clumps out of litter box, puts it in a
                    bag she finds on the countertop, ties it up and puts
                    it in the garbage pail.)

                              TAMMY
                         (calling)
Those sausages you sent over last week were delicious, by
the way! My brother was lucky to get even one!

                    (TAMMY seems contented, as she reminisces about the
                    sausages. There is a long silent pause. Then her
                    expression changes somewhat to worry.)

                              TAMMY
                         (calling)
Grandma? Are you o.k.?
                         (sniffing at the air, then to stuffed animal
                         cat staring)
Yeah, I smell it, too. That's nasty, huh?

                    (TAMMY notices that the oven is on. Goes over to it
                    to shut it off.)

                              TAMMY
                         (calling)
I'm turning off the oven, Grandma!
                         (to self)
Something smells god-awful! Ew!
                         (calling, again)
Whatever you were cooking, I think it's done!

                    (She shuts oven off, opens oven door, puts on an oven
                    mit, and pulls out a baking dish. There is a roasted
                    animal in the baking dish. It was a real cat.)

                    (TAMMY screams at the sight of the cat in the baking
                    dish, and she drops it to the floor.)

                    (She backs up into shelving behind her. From a shelf
                    above, a dead, bloodied real cat falls on her head,
                    then bounces off onto the floor.)

                    (TAMMY sends out another chilling scream at this
                    sight.)

                              TAMMY
Oh, my God! What's happening here?!

                        TAMMY (cont'd)
                          (calling)
Grandma! I-I-I'm gonna be late for class! I'll call you
later, o.k.? Grandma! I'm *leaving!!!*

        (TAMMY runs to the front door, opens it. She gasps at
        the sight of her grandmother standing in the doorway.)

        (GRANDMA stands at attention, a strangely satisfied
        expression on her face. She has blood on her clothing,
        and she holds the bloody head of one of her cats in
        one hand, a bloody knife in the other.)

                          GRANDMA
I've been so lonely lately, Dear. Won't you stay for lunch?

(TAMMY's frantic last scream ends the scene. BLACKOUT.)

                        CURTAIN

"THE CYLINDER"

A Radio Play Thriller

By Karen Carson

"THE CYLINDER"

NARRATOR: JEREMY and SCOTT, two teenagers, 13 and 15, respectively, love their dune-buggy outings in the hot desert sun of Death Valley. They never tire of the excitement of the sand flying all around them, and into their faces, as they zoom through the soft mountains of sand, not a care in the world – no rules, no streetlights, no speed limits. No limits at all.

But this bright, hot afternoon, they've decided to park their dune-buggies and take a little exploratory stroll. I think they might regret it.

(Sound of heavy breathing, 5 times, then a gasp.)

JEREMY: Scott! Is that you?

SCOTT: Yeah. I'm here, Jeremy.

JEREMY: Where are we?

SCOTT: Not sure.

JEREMY: How did we get here?

SCOTT: I don't know. I don't remember.

JEREMY: I can't see you.

SCOTT: Yeah. It's really dark.

JEREMY: You got a flashlight? Or a lighter?

SCOTT: No. Hey, I think I got some matches.

JEREMY: Hurry, will ya? I'm freakin' out.

SCOTT: Just take it easy. O.k., I found 'em. Wait. Let me … o.k.

(Sound of match being struck.)

JEREMY: Wo. What is this place?

SCOTT: I don't know.

JEREMY: It's all metal. The walls are metal. What could this be?

SCOTT: A safe?

JEREMY: A bomb shelter?

SCOTT: But we were dune-buggyin'. Who would have a safe in the desert?

JEREMY: Or a bomb shelter.

SCOTT: We must've fallen in. Let's try to find the exit.

(Sound of them scuffling around.)

SCOTT: Look. The floor is metal, too.

JEREMY: Where's a door?

SCOTT: Wait. I'm lookin'. I don't see any … Ouch!

JEREMY: What happened?! It's dark again!

(They stop scuffling.)

SCOTT: The match went out.

JEREMY: Well, light another one. We gotta find a doorway out.

SCOTT: Yeah. But I only have two matches left.

JEREMY: What?!

SCOTT: What a time to quit smokin', huh?

JEREMY: Yeah, right.

SCOTT: Well, I could use one right now, I'll tell ya!

JEREMY: Look. Why don't you hold onto me, and we'll feel around the walls for a way out.

SCOTT: What do I have to hold onto ya for? You can hear me breathin', can't ya?

JEREMY: *(Disappointed)* Yeah.

SCOTT: O.k. I'll hold on.

JEREMY: We got a wall over here. It seems to go on.

(Sound of their feet scuffling the metal floor)

SCOTT: Is it curving?

JEREMY: I think it is.

SCOTT: So, it's like a round room? A round, metal room?

JEREMY: I don't know. It just keeps curvin' around.
Around and around!

SCOTT: I wonder how big it is.

JEREMY: Still curving. Still curving.

SCOTT: No doorway yet?

JEREMY: No. Nothing.

SCOTT: Hey! How do we know if we're not right back where
we started from?

JEREMY: O.k., I'm freakin' out again!

SCOTT: O.k., o.k. Take it easy. Listen. I'm gonna light
another match. Just look around fast, o.k.?

JEREMY: Yeah, yeah.

SCOTT: O.k., ready?

JEREMY: Yeah, yeah.

(Sound of match being struck.)

(They both sigh.)

SCOTT: *(A little nervous laughter)* I never missed the
light so much.

JEREMY: Me, neither.

SCOTT: O.k., look up. Maybe there's an opening above.

JEREMY: Yeah, hold the light up there.

SCOTT: I'm holdin' it up.

JEREMY: I don't see any ceiling.

SCOTT: I'm holdin' it as high as I can, I'm standin' on my toes.

JEREMY: No ceiling. Maybe you can stand on my shoulders.

SCOTT: The match won't last that long.

JEREMY: Oh. O.k., light up the wall again.

SCOTT: Alright. What's this?

JEREMY: Looks like a drawing. Or like an etching … in the metal.

SCOTT: … Of a man in a round

BOTH: … metal room.

(Silent pause)

SCOTT: Yowww!

JEREMY: What happened?! What is it?!

SCOTT: The match burned my finger again. Damn! In the same place!

JEREMY: You say you only have one match left?

SCOTT: Yeah. How 'bout you? You got any?

JEREMY: No. I don't have any.

SCOTT: Alright. Well, I'm gonna have to light the last one to see what we were lookin' at.

JEREMY: Yeah. Maybe it's a clue. Maybe it'll tell us where we are.

SCOTT: But, wait. Maybe … Should we just feel around a little bit more? Try to find the doorway?

JEREMY: We might lose our place with the picture on the wall. Then we won't have any more light to see it again.

SCOTT: Oh. Yeah, you're right. O.k.

JEREMY: Wait! Let's be ready.

SCOTT: Well, I can't be more ready than with my eyes open.

JEREMY: Oh. Alright.

SCOTT: Ready?

JEREMY: Yeah. Eyes open.

(Sound of match being struck.)

SCOTT: O.k., o.k., there it is! It's a man in a round room.

JEREMY: Move it over a little. There!

SCOTT: The room has a cover on it. Like half-way closed. (beat) And way up!

JEREMY: And over a little. There!

SCOTT: O.k. What's this?

JEREMY: The round room is closed, with the man inside, and … and …

SCOTT: And he's being lifted up toward a space ship.

JEREMY: Looks like a flying saucer. (Panicky)

SCOTT: Ouch! Damn! Again!

JEREMY: Scott. Are we in that round room? Are we …?

SCOTT: What?! No! No, of course not …!

(Suddenly, the sound of a large metal object high above them is slowly closing off the cylindrical metal room.)

JEREMY: Scott!   Scott!

SCOTT: I'm here, Jeremy!

JEREMY: What'll we do?!

SCOTT: I don't think we can …!   I don't know!

JEREMY: What'll we do?!

SCOTT: I don't know!   I don't know!

(BOTH of them scream "Help!   Help!" in horror.)

(Sound of metal clang – it has closed off the room, as well as very suddenly silencing their screams.)

(Sound of accelerating quiet computerized motor, of sorts, pitch gets higher and higher, until it "zaps", and then suddenly stops.)

THE END

"THE PARTING"

A Short Dramatic Play

by, Karen Carson

"THE PARTING"

SCENE ONE
(Interior of a farmhouse, kitchen area.)

The house is set up in a quaint country style. There
are two cups of coffee at the kitchen table, accom-
panied by a napkin and spoon each. There is also
sugar and cream in the middle of the table.

CHARLOTTE is tickled as she peers out the window into
their backyard at HENRY, who is feeding the chickens.

Note: as the characters speak, they never look at
each other directly, although they do look in their
direction at times.

                    CHARLOTTE
                (looking out window)
Oh, he loves those chickens! He feeds those hens before he
feeds himself his own breakfast!

HENRY enters with coffee cans he used for the chicken
feed, places them on the countertop.

                    CHARLOTTE
You feed those chickens before you feed yourself.

                    HENRY
Damned birds!

HENRY sits at kitchen table, opens up newspaper.

                    CHARLOTTE
                (cheerfully)
Oh, you know you love them birds! I bet we're about out of
cat food, too.

                    HENRY
                (reads a headline aloud)
"George Hanley caught with fingers in the kitty." Ha!

                    CHARLOTTE
"Ha" is right!

                        HENRY
Whaddya know about that?!

                        CHARLOTTE
I knew he was embezzling money from Carl's store, I think
he's been doin' it a long time!

                        HENRY
Stupid basterd!
            (turns pages)

                        CHARLOTTE
Serves him right, I should say.
            (sips coffee)
Oh, yuck! Henry!

                        HENRY
            (beat, sighs)
You always like sugar in your coffee.

                        CHARLOTTE
Yeah, but not this much!

    HENRY turns pages of newspaper, 'til something catches
    his attention. He stops, puts down paper.

                        HENRY
We need milk.

                        CHARLOTTE
I told you that yesterday. You never listen to me.
            (sips coffee again)
Yech! Oh, I'm done with this! Henry, that's gotta be the
worst cup of coffee you ever made for me in thirty years!
Yuck!
            (gets up to exit kitchen)
Better check to see what else we need. I'm gonna go powder
my nose. Put cat food on the list.

    CHARLOTTE leaves the kitchen. HENRY seems to be in a
    daze.

    He looks at newspaper page. He is saddened, puts his
    head down.

                    HENRY
               (to self)
We need milk.

          HENRY goes to the refrigerator. He is distracted,
          walks kind of like a zombie.

                    HENRY
               (peering blankly into refrigerator)
What else do we need?
               (calling out, not looking in any
                particular direction)
You're better at this than I am!

          HENRY slams refrigerator and sits again., head in
          hands.

          CHARLOTTE comes back into kitchen, purse in hand.

                    CHARLOTTE
I told you, Henry. We need cat food.
               (looks through her purse)
Well, this is as good as the makeup will let me get today.

                    HENRY
               (looks at cat dish)
Oh, yeah. Cat food. We need cat food.

                    CHARLOTTE
               (taking compact out of purse)
Finally!

                    HENRY
We need milk and cat food.

                    CHARLOTTE
               (looking into compact mirror from her purse)
Maybe I'll get a new hairstyle. Whaddya think?

          HENRY begins to weep.

                    CHARLOTTE
O.k.! I won't spend the money! Geez!
               (scoffs, puts compact back in purse)

                    HENRY
Oh, Charlotte!

                            CHARLOTTE
                 (leans down, puts arm around him)
What?! What is it, honey? Are we that strapped for cash?

                            HENRY
We need milk. And we need cat food. And I don't know what
else.

                            CHARLOTTE
                 (straightens up)
Well, is that any reason to act crazy? Why so sad, Henry?
You can tell me.

                            HENRY
What else? You know what else we need.
                 (puts his head in his hands again)

                            CHARLOTTE
O.k., is this a riddle now? Henry, I don't like games, you
know that.

                            HENRY
I just don't know where to look.

                            CHARLOTTE
Well, … in the cabinets! O.k., I'll take a look. Geez!
Don't stress out like this.

                            HENRY
I don't wanna go!

                            CHARLOTTE
                 (sarcastically)
What a surprise!
                 (goes to refrigerator)
You couldn't just tell me that? Look, the milk can last
maybe another day. And we'll give the cats some tuna, or
something. We'll go tomorrow.

                            HENRY
                 (angrily)
Oh, Charlotte! We need milk! And we need cat food!!

                            CHARLOTTE
O.k., you're startin' to get me nervous now. What is going
on?!

HENRY leaves kitchen.

                    CHARLOTTE
You know, you're freakin' me out!
          (calling)
Henry!
          (pause, calling)
So, are we goin', or not?!

    CHARLOTTE sits at table, sighs.

                    CHARLOTTE
          (calls out)
Well, I'm ready, if you decide to go!
          (long pause, notices newspaper article,
          surprised, joyful at first)
Hey, look! My picture!
          (pause)
Why is my picture … in the paper? Why is my picture … in
the obituaries? Oh, no! No!
          (stands up)

    HENRY enters kitchen, places keys on the table, takes
    a deep breath. Her eyes are on him now.

                    CHARLOTTE
Henry! What's this all about, Henry?!

    HENRY is gathering his thoughts.

                    CHARLOTTE
Henry! Answer me! How did this happen?!

    HENRY looks down, holding back his tears.

                    CHARLOTTE
The paper says I died a week ago. Henry, …

    HENRY picks up coffee cups and spoons, pauses.

                    CHARLOTTE
You made me coffee.

    HENRY brings cups and spoons to the sink, rinses them
    out.

                    CHARLOTTE
              (starts laughing, then cries)
I guess old habits are hard to break!

CHARLOTTE puts her hands over her face for a moment of
grief.

     HENRY comes back to table, takes keys.

                      HENRY
Milk. And cat food.
              (stops, looks around)
What else?

                    CHARLOTTE
Honey!

                      HENRY
I don't know. I don't know, I don't know!
              (pause)
Whatever else is not important right now.

                    CHARLOTTE
That's right! That's right, Henry!

     HENRY leaves with the keys, closing and locking door
     behind him.

                    CHARLOTTE
You just do what you have to do. Don't worry about trivial
things. Life is too short, and …
              (pause)
I-I-I'll just … wait here. Right here. I'll be right
here … when you get back.

     CHARLOTTE sits facing the door. Looks down, shakes
     her head in disbelief.

                    CURTAIN

19176023R00024

Printed in Poland
by Amazon Fulfillment
Poland Sp. z o.o., Wrocław